Manage
Your Week
Like a Pro!

Weekly Planner

Activinotes

Activinotes

DAILY JOURNALS, PLANNERS, NOTEBOOKS AND OTHER BLANK BOOKS

Notes

_____

_____

_____

_____

_____

_____

_____

_____

_____

_____

_____

MONDAY	TUESDAY	WEDNESDAY	To Do List

THURSDAY	FRIDAY	SATURDAY	To Buy List

SUNDAY			To Do List

Notes & Jots

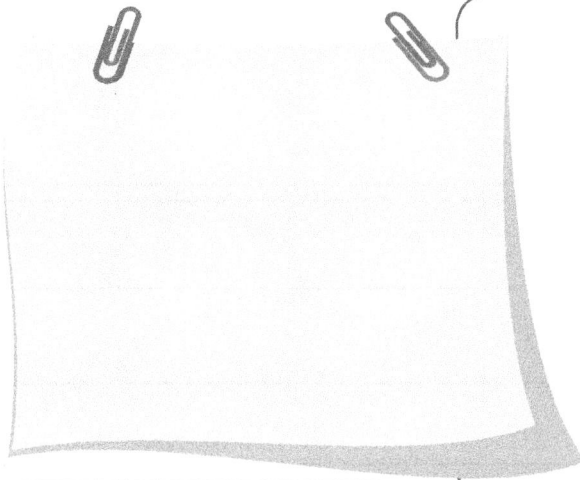

Notes

MONDAY	TUESDAY	WEDNESDAY	To Do List

THURSDAY	FRIDAY	SATURDAY	To Buy List

SUNDAY	To Do List

Notes & Jots

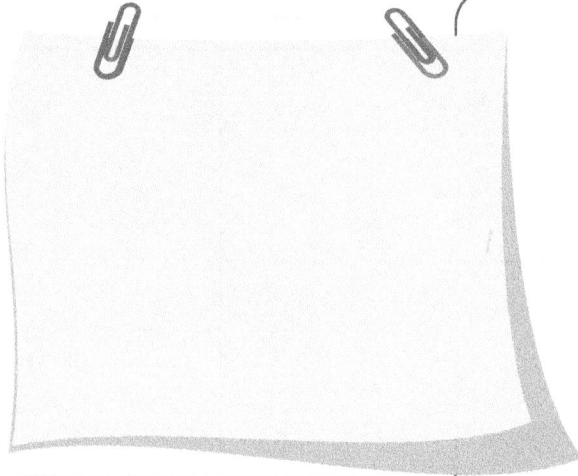

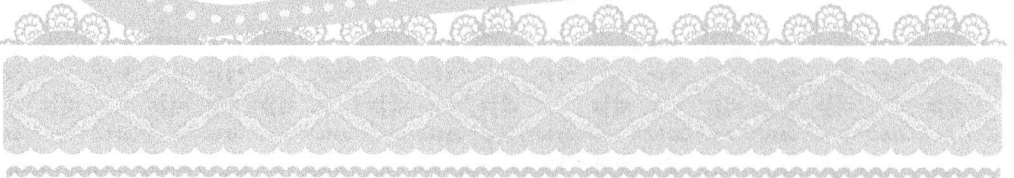

Notes

_____
_____

_____

_____

_____

_____

_____

_____

_____

_____

_____

MONDAY	TUESDAY	WEDNESDAY	To Do List

THURSDAY	FRIDAY	SATURDAY	To Buy List

SUNDAY			To Do List

Notes & Jots

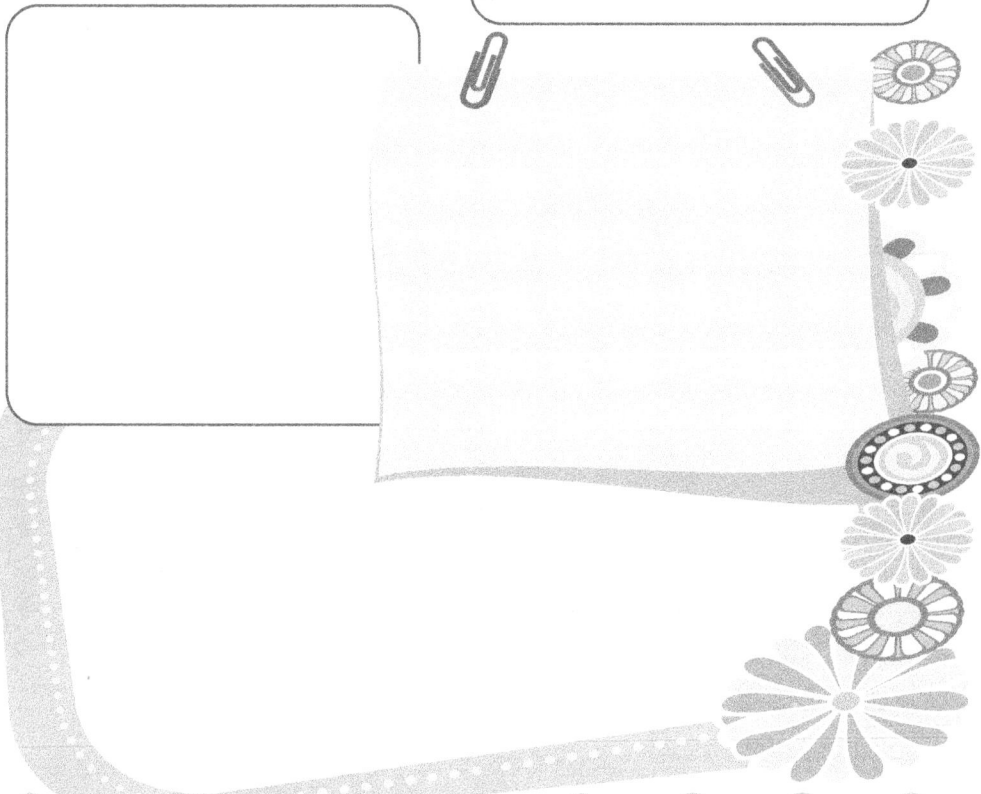

Notes

_____

_____

_____

_____

_____

_____

_____

_____

_____

_____

_____

MONDAY	TUESDAY	WEDNESDAY	To Do List

THURSDAY	FRIDAY	SATURDAY	To Buy List

SUNDAY			To Do List

Notes & Jots

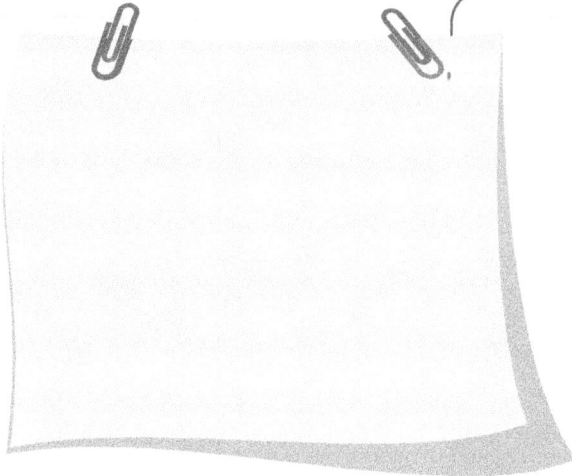

Notes

_____
_____

_____

_____

_____

_____

_____

_____

_____

_____

_____

MONDAY	TUESDAY	WEDNESDAY	To Do List

THURSDAY	FRIDAY	SATURDAY	To Buy List

SUNDAY			To Do List

Notes & Jots

Notes

_____

_____

_____

_____

_____

_____

_____

_____

_____

_____

_____

MONDAY	TUESDAY	WEDNESDAY	To Do List

THURSDAY	FRIDAY	SATURDAY	To Buy List

SUNDAY	To Do List

Notes & Jots

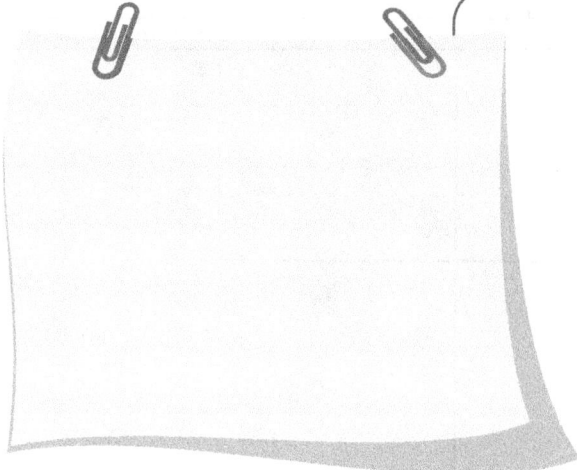

Notes

_____

_____

_____

_____

_____

_____

_____

_____

_____

_____

_____

MONDAY	TUESDAY	WEDNESDAY	To Do List

THURSDAY	FRIDAY	SATURDAY	To Buy List

SUNDAY	To Do List

Notes & Jots

Notes

_____

_____

_____

_____

_____

_____

_____

_____

_____

_____

_____

Manage your week like a Pro!

MONDAY	TUESDAY	WEDNESDAY	To Do List

THURSDAY	FRIDAY	SATURDAY	To Buy List

SUNDAY			To Do List

Notes & Jots

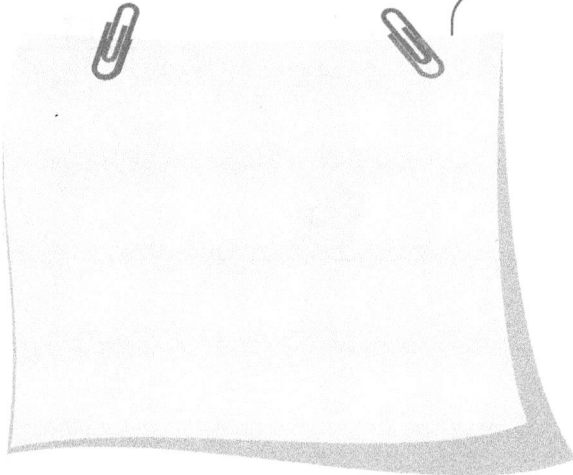

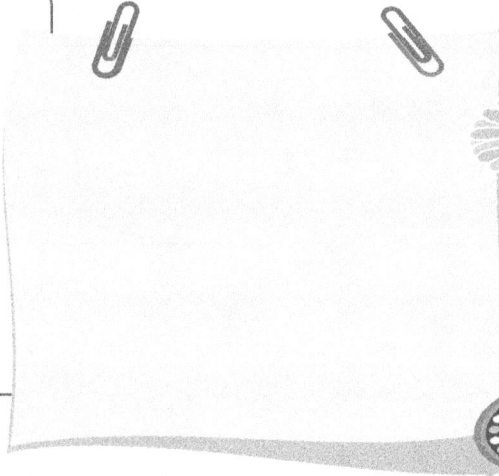

Notes

_____
_____

_____

_____

_____

_____

_____

_____

_____

_____

_____

_____

MONDAY	TUESDAY	WEDNESDAY	To Do List

THURSDAY	FRIDAY	SATURDAY	To Buy List

SUNDAY			To Do List

Notes & Jots

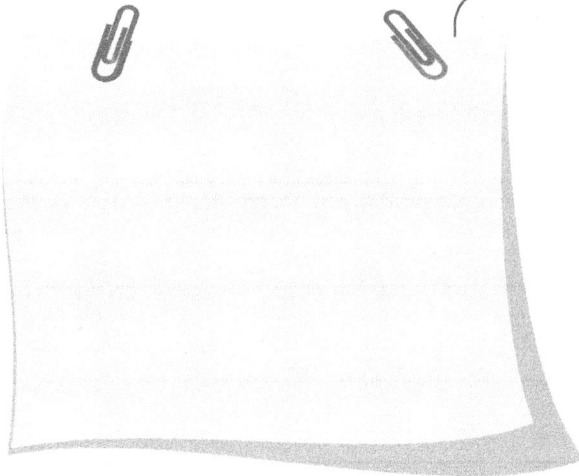

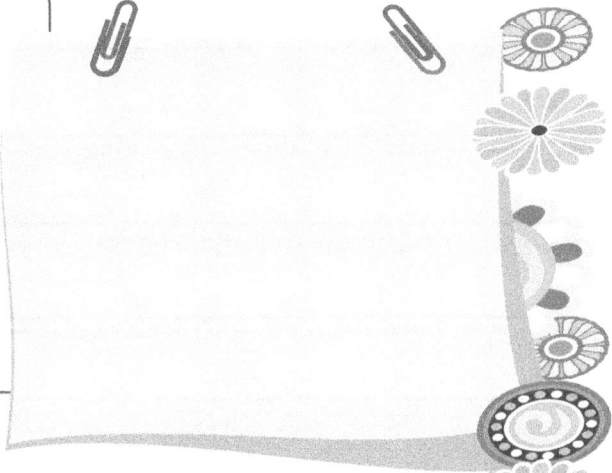

Notes

_____

_____

_____

_____

_____

_____

_____

_____

_____

_____

_____

MONDAY	TUESDAY	WEDNESDAY	To Do List

THURSDAY	FRIDAY	SATURDAY	To Buy List

SUNDAY	To Do List

Notes & Jots

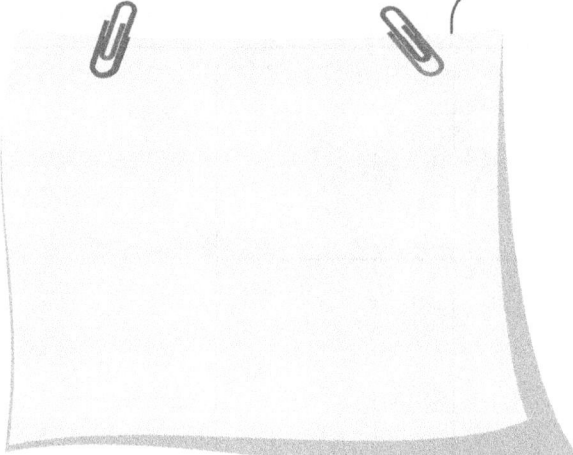

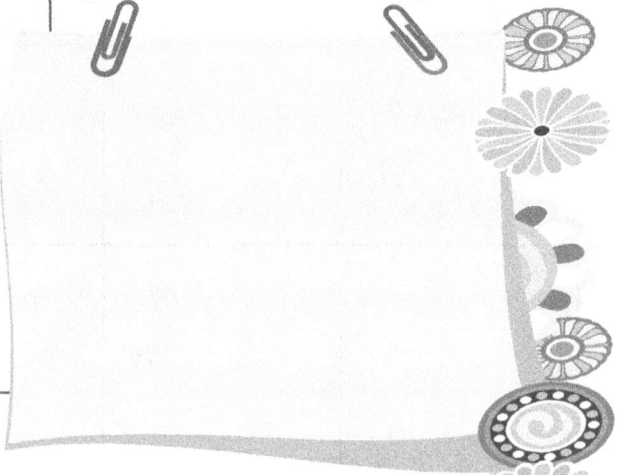

Notes

MONDAY	TUESDAY	WEDNESDAY	To Do List

THURSDAY	FRIDAY	SATURDAY	To Buy List

SUNDAY	To Do List

Notes & Jots

Notes

_____
_____
_____
_____
_____
_____
_____
_____
_____
_____
_____

MONDAY	TUESDAY	WEDNESDAY	To Do List

THURSDAY	FRIDAY	SATURDAY	To Buy List

SUNDAY			To Do List

Notes & Jots

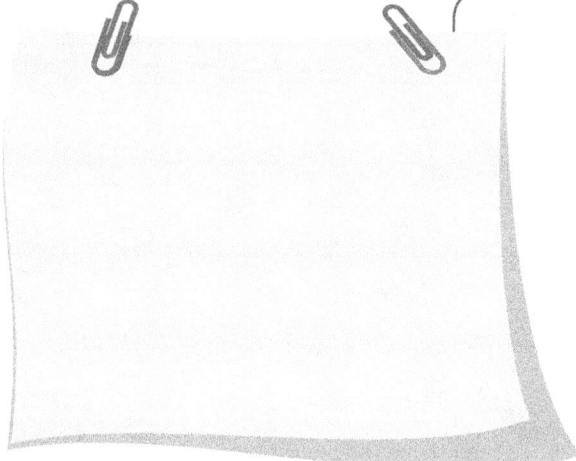

Notes

_____

_____

_____

_____

_____

_____

_____

_____

_____

_____

_____

MONDAY	TUESDAY	WEDNESDAY	To Do List

THURSDAY	FRIDAY	SATURDAY	To Buy List

SUNDAY		To Do List

Notes & Jots

Notes

_____
_____
_____
_____
_____
_____
_____
_____
_____
_____
_____

MONDAY	TUESDAY	WEDNESDAY	To Do List

THURSDAY	FRIDAY	SATURDAY	To Buy List

SUNDAY		To Do List

Notes & Jots

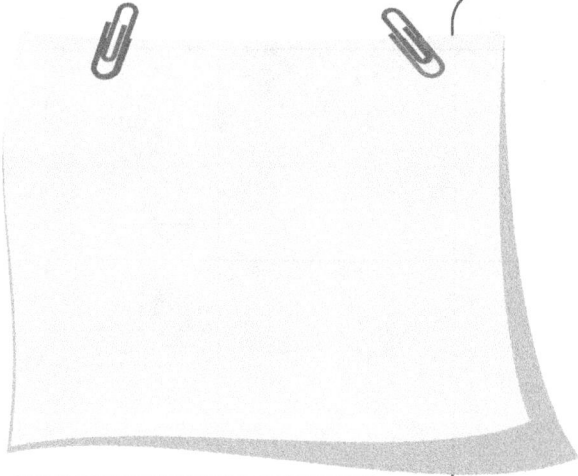

Notes

MONDAY	TUESDAY	WEDNESDAY	To Do List

THURSDAY	FRIDAY	SATURDAY	To Buy List

SUNDAY			To Do List

Notes & Jots

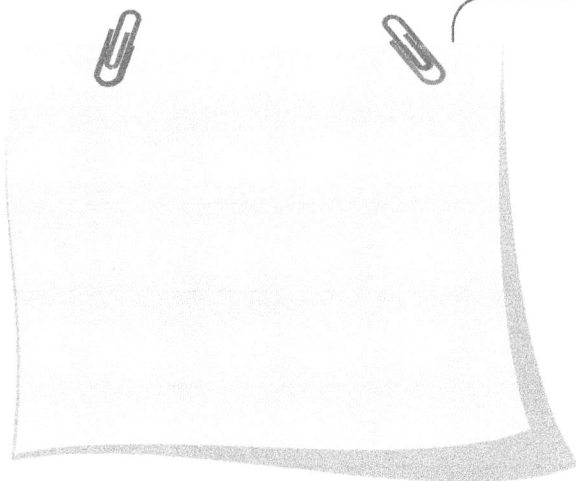

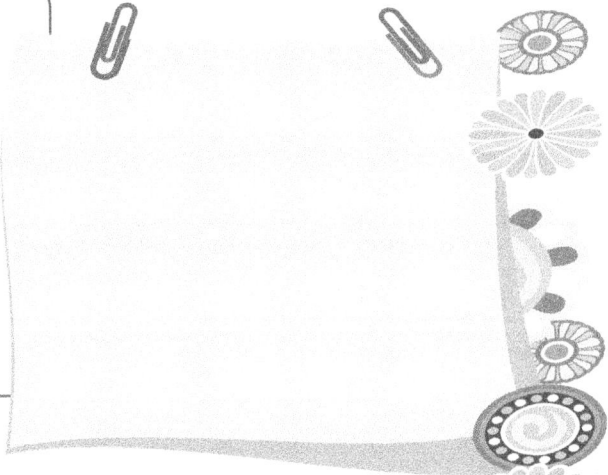

Notes

_____

_____

_____

_____

_____

_____

_____

_____

_____

_____

_____

MONDAY	TUESDAY	WEDNESDAY	To Do List

THURSDAY	FRIDAY	SATURDAY	To Buy List

SUNDAY			To Do List

Notes & Jots

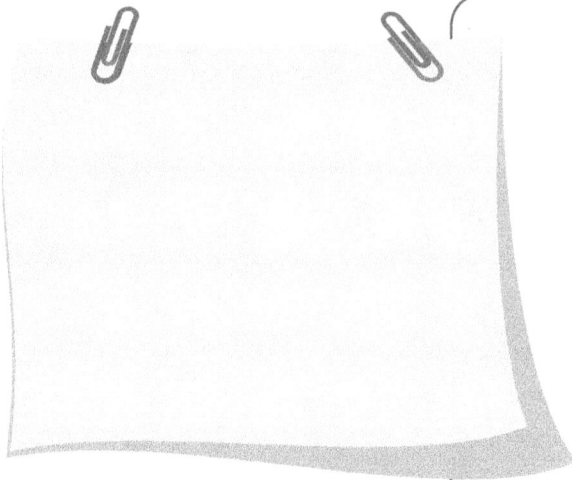

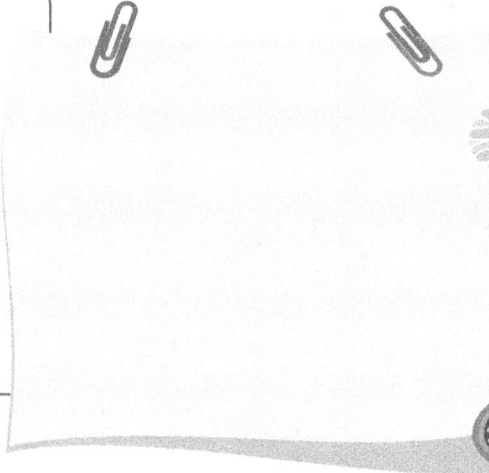

Notes

_____
_____

_____

_____

_____

_____

_____

_____

_____

_____

_____

MONDAY	TUESDAY	WEDNESDAY	To Do List

THURSDAY	FRIDAY	SATURDAY	To Buy List

SUNDAY	To Do List

Notes & Jots

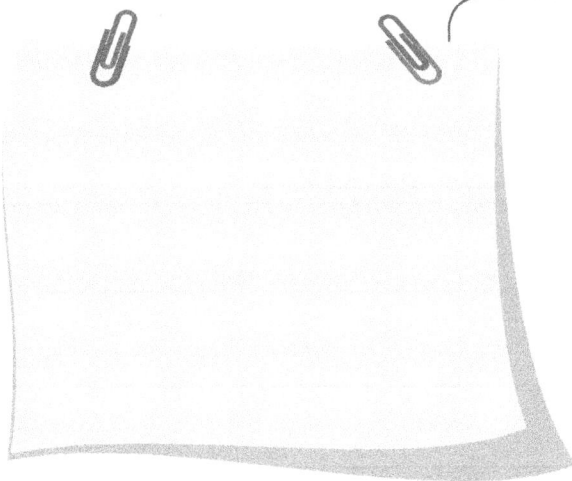

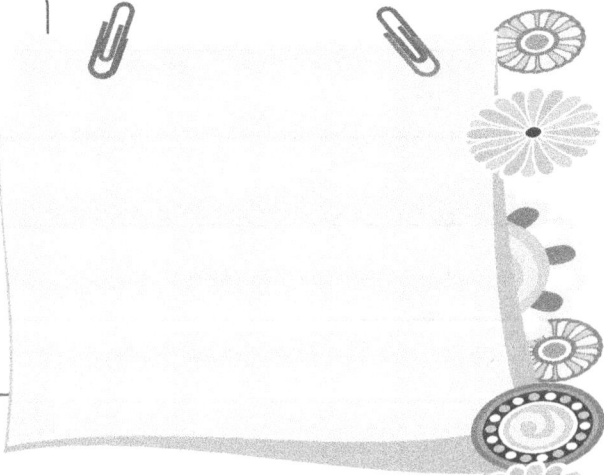

Notes

_____

_____

_____

_____

_____

_____

_____

_____

_____

_____

_____

_____

MONDAY	TUESDAY	WEDNESDAY	To Do List

THURSDAY	FRIDAY	SATURDAY	To Buy List

SUNDAY			To Do List

Notes & Jots

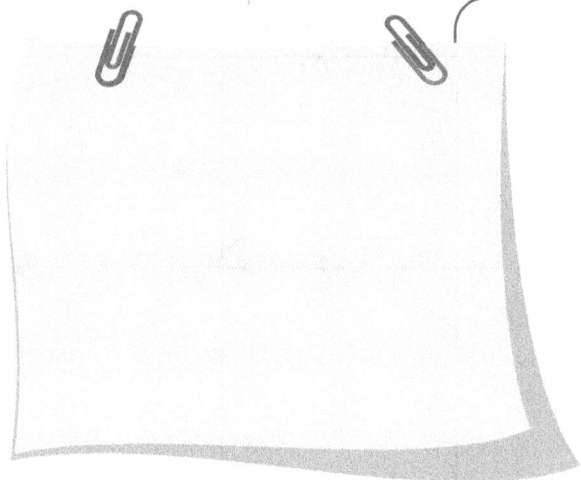
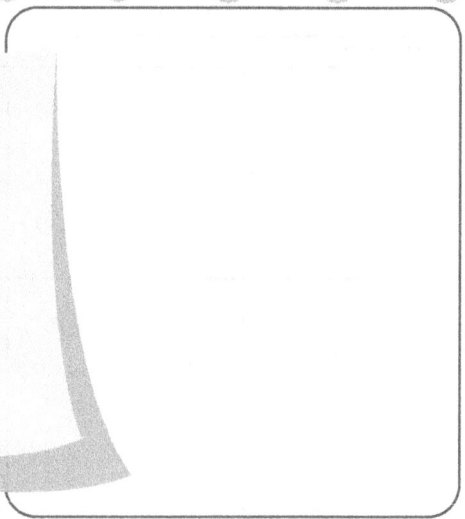

Notes

_____
_____

_____

_____

_____

_____

_____

_____

_____

_____

_____

MONDAY	TUESDAY	WEDNESDAY	To Do List

THURSDAY	FRIDAY	SATURDAY	To Buy List

SUNDAY			To Do List

Notes & Jots

Notes

_____

_____

_____

_____

_____

_____

_____

_____

_____

_____

_____

MONDAY	TUESDAY	WEDNESDAY	To Do List

THURSDAY	FRIDAY	SATURDAY	To Buy List

SUNDAY			To Do List

Notes & Jots

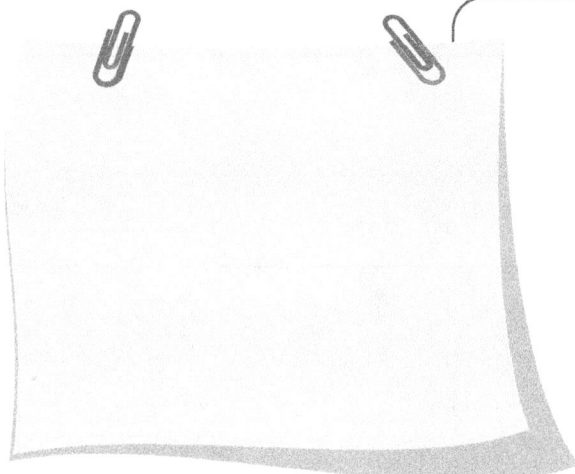

Notes

_____

_____

_____

_____

_____

_____

_____

_____

_____

_____

_____

MONDAY	TUESDAY	WEDNESDAY	To Do List

THURSDAY	FRIDAY	SATURDAY	To Buy List

SUNDAY			To Do List

Notes & Jots

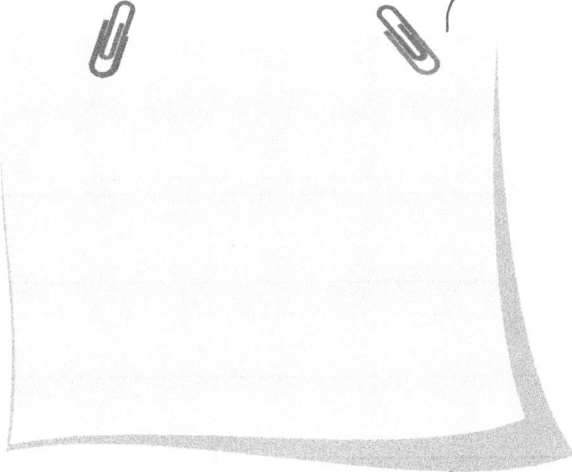

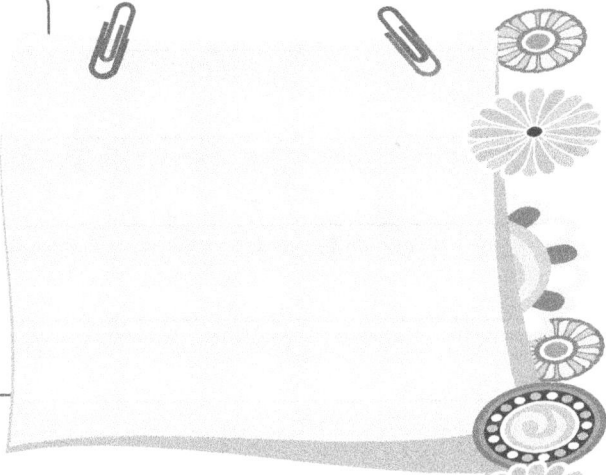

Notes

MONDAY	TUESDAY	WEDNESDAY	To Do List

THURSDAY	FRIDAY	SATURDAY	To Buy List

SUNDAY			To Do List

Notes & Jots

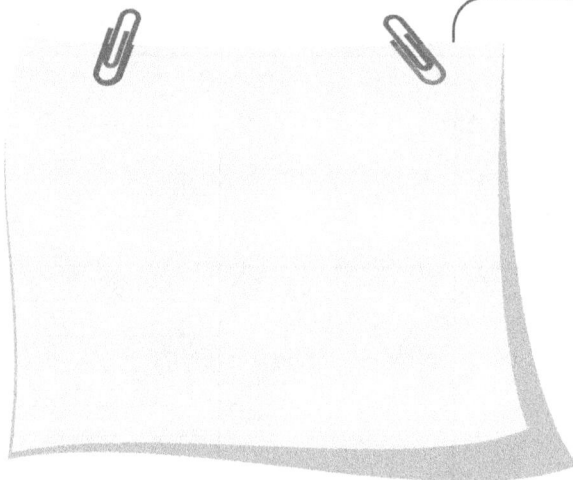

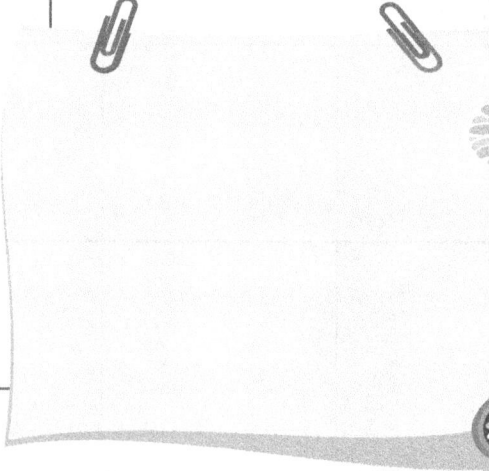

Notes

_____

_____

_____

_____

_____

_____

_____

_____

_____

_____

_____

MONDAY	TUESDAY	WEDNESDAY	To Do List

THURSDAY	FRIDAY	SATURDAY	To Buy List

SUNDAY		To Do List

Notes & Jots

Notes

_____

_____

_____

_____

_____

_____

_____

_____

_____

_____

_____

MONDAY	TUESDAY	WEDNESDAY	To Do List

THURSDAY	FRIDAY	SATURDAY	To Buy List

SUNDAY			To Do List

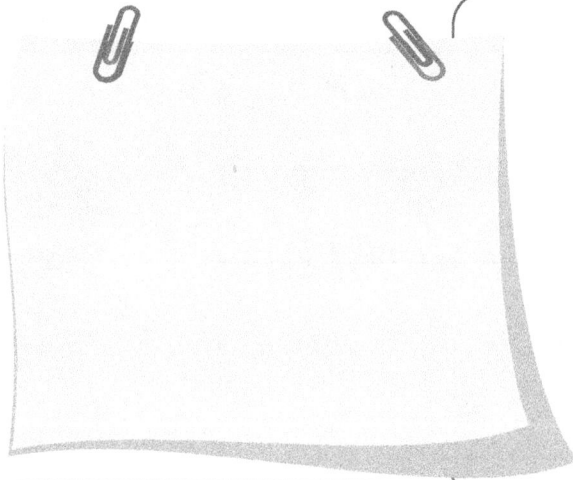

Notes

_____

_____

_____

_____

_____

_____

_____

_____

_____

_____

_____

MONDAY	TUESDAY	WEDNESDAY	To Do List

THURSDAY	FRIDAY	SATURDAY	To Buy List

SUNDAY			To Do List

Notes & Jots

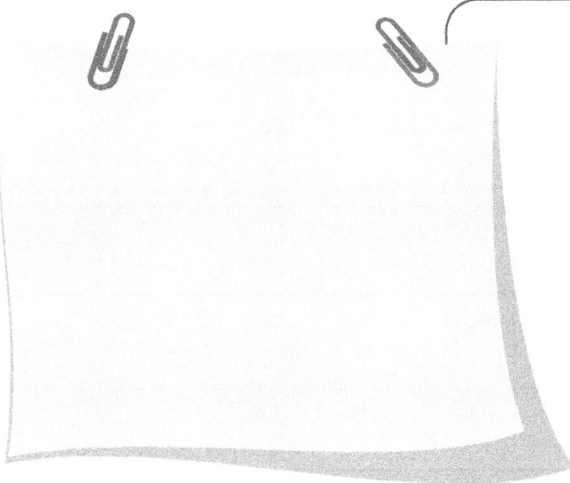

Notes

MONDAY	TUESDAY	WEDNESDAY	To Do List

THURSDAY	FRIDAY	SATURDAY	To Buy List

SUNDAY			To Do List

Notes & Jots

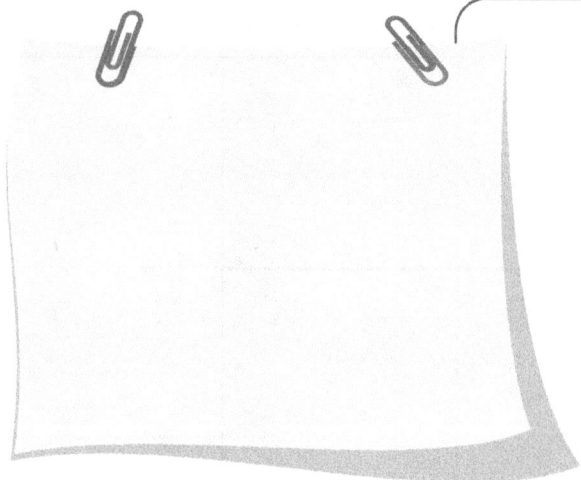

Notes

MONDAY	TUESDAY	WEDNESDAY	To Do List

THURSDAY	FRIDAY	SATURDAY	To Buy List

SUNDAY	To Do List

Notes & Jots

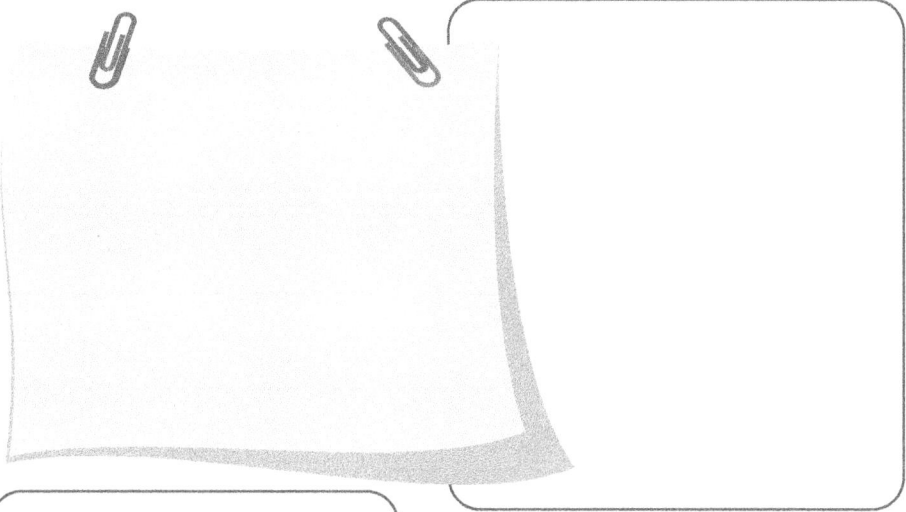

Notes

_____

_____

_____

_____

_____

_____

_____

_____

_____

_____

_____

_____

MONDAY	TUESDAY	WEDNESDAY	To Do List

THURSDAY	FRIDAY	SATURDAY	To Buy List

SUNDAY			To Do List

Notes & Jots

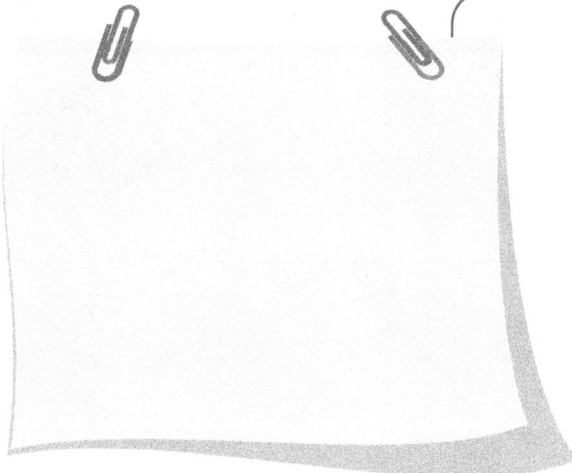

Notes

_____

_____

_____

_____

_____

_____

_____

_____

_____

_____

_____

MONDAY	TUESDAY	WEDNESDAY	To Do List

THURSDAY	FRIDAY	SATURDAY	To Buy List

SUNDAY			To Do List

Notes & Jots

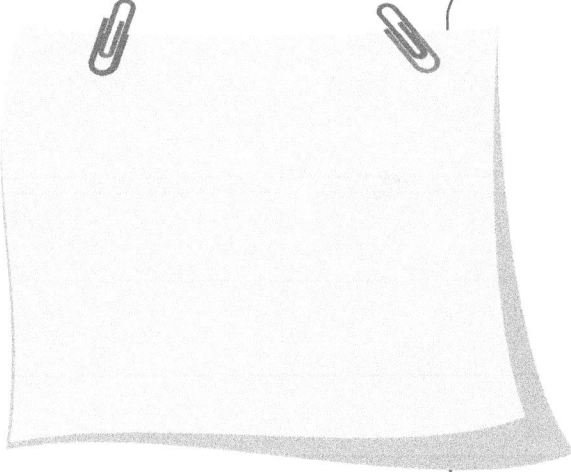

Notes

MONDAY	TUESDAY	WEDNESDAY	To Do List

THURSDAY	FRIDAY	SATURDAY	To Buy List

SUNDAY		To Do List

Notes & Jots

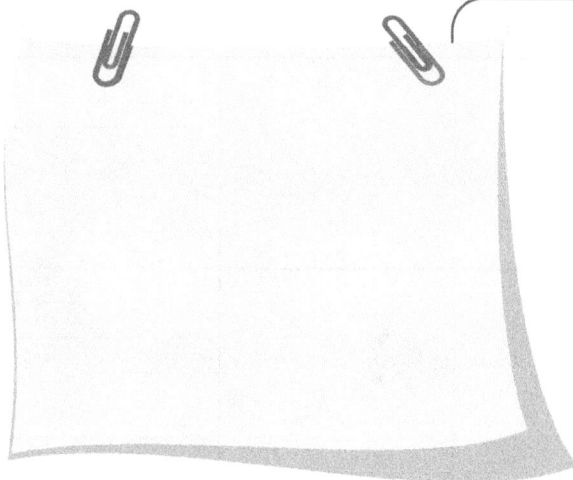

Notes

_____
_____
_____
_____
_____
_____
_____
_____
_____
_____
_____
_____

MONDAY	TUESDAY	WEDNESDAY	To Do List

THURSDAY	FRIDAY	SATURDAY	To Buy List

SUNDAY	To Do List

Notes & Jots

Notes

MONDAY	TUESDAY	WEDNESDAY	To Do List

THURSDAY	FRIDAY	SATURDAY	To Buy List

SUNDAY			To Do List

Notes & Jots

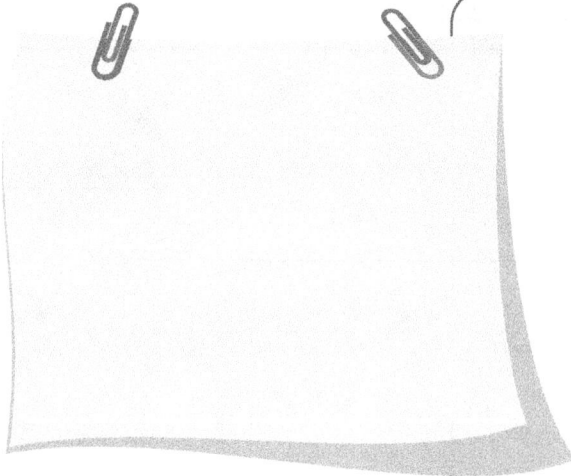

Notes

MONDAY	TUESDAY	WEDNESDAY	To Do List

THURSDAY	FRIDAY	SATURDAY	To Buy List

SUNDAY		To Do List

Notes & Jots

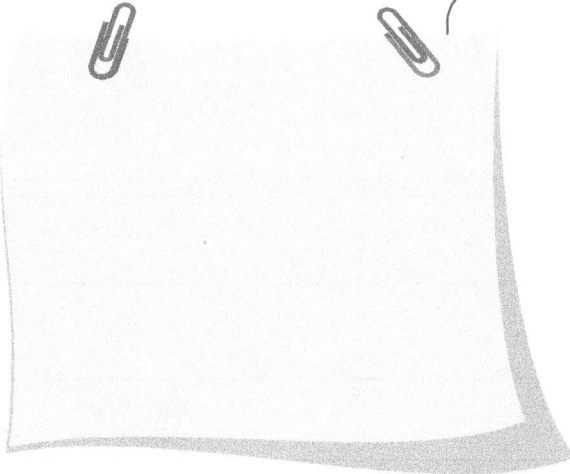

Notes

_____

_____

_____

_____

_____

_____

_____

_____

_____

_____

_____

MONDAY	TUESDAY	WEDNESDAY	To Do List

THURSDAY	FRIDAY	SATURDAY	To Buy List

SUNDAY		To Do List

Notes & Jots

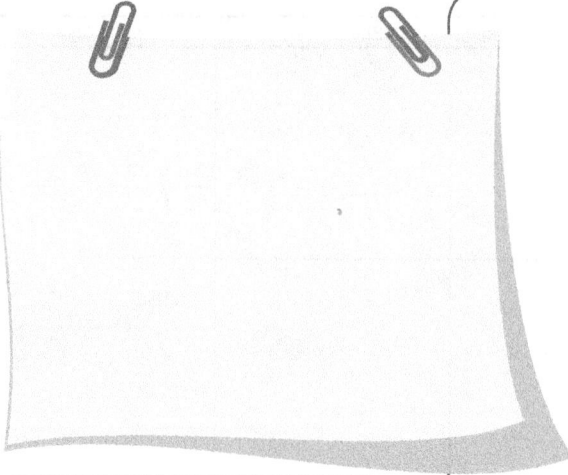

Notes

_____

_____

_____

_____

_____

_____

_____

_____

_____

_____

_____

www.ingramcontent.com/pod-product-compliance
Lightning Source LLC
Chambersburg PA
CBHW081335090426
42737CB00017B/3148